MARY McCARTHY: A BIBLIOGRAPHY

MARY McCARTHY

A BIBLIOGRAPHY

By
Sherli Evens Goldman

HARCOURT, BRACE & WORLD, INC., NEW YORK

First edition
Library of Congress Catalog Card Number: 68-12574
Printed in the United States of America

To the memory of my father
and mother

INTRODUCTORY NOTE

LIKE most bibliographies, this one of Mary McCarthy seeks completeness. It is an account of the author's publishing history. What I have attempted to do is to cite every appearance in print of Miss McCarthy's work. I am aware of the wide margin for error in such an undertaking—indeed, such is the bibliographer's inevitable lot.

Two omissions known to me are Miss McCarthy's prize-winning essay, "The Irish in American History," written when she was ten years old, and possibly published in the Minneapolis *Tribune* or a Catholic publication; and her College Entrance Examination Board essay, published anonymously in a CEEB journal of the early nineteen-thirties as the example of an essay scoring in the 90–100 percentile. I have tried without success to find these two important pieces of juvenilia.

I have examined all of the periodicals in which there are contributions by Mary McCarthy, utilizing largely the resources of the University of California, Los Angeles, Research Library. Where I have been unable to examine a book, my information comes from the publishers or from other authorities. These titles are starred in sections A and B. However, since the information on foreign translations comes chiefly from the publishers, rather than from the books themselves, I have omitted stars in this section. The reader may assume that I have not seen any particular foreign translation. Editions whose publishers I was unable to get in touch with and which were not listed either in the national bibliographies or in the *Index Translationum* are not included. Where I do have information, even though the book may not yet be in print, I have tried to indicate it (as with the Yugoslavian edition of *The Group*).

Introductory Note

My model has been Donald Gallup, *T. S. Eliot: A Bibliography* (Harcourt, Brace and Company, 1953). I have used Professor Gallup's divisions and indexing method, which seem to me eminently easy to use.

The descriptive system I have used is also based on Professor Gallup's, which is itself a modification of that used by the American Library Association. By this method all leaves are accounted for, whether printed or blank. When the preliminary unnumbered leaves in a volume do not count up to the first numbered page, they are specified in the collation; e.g., "1 blank leaf, 5 leaves, 3–304 pp." If the collation read simply "3–304 pp." the reader would know that only one unnumbered leaf preceded the numbered pages. When the printed text either begins or ends on an unnumbered page, the number (inferred from the verso or recto of the page on which it appears) is given in brackets. Thus, the collation "[3]–304 pp." means that the first page number is 4 although the text begins on the recto.

In its original form this bibliography had separate classifications for fiction and nonfiction. This led to problems. For example, "Yellowstone Park," which appears in the autobiographical *Memories of a Catholic Girlhood,* won an O. Henry short-story prize in 1957. Miss McCarthy's own views on these problems of classification, expressed in a letter to me, set forth the dilemma: "Whenever one classifies one gets into Talmudic puzzles. It happens to me every time I decide to rearrange my library: does Racine go under French literature or under drama, and what do you do about a collection, say Swift, of prose and poetry—does it go under poetry or English literature? Where does the *Kinsey Report* belong? In the medical department or under social history? I can never make up my mind about letters. Do they follow the author's works, which is OK for Byron or George Eliot, or do they go on a shelf that includes gossip and autobiography—memoirs? Some people list everything alphabetically by authors, but that makes it hard to find a book that you remember more by subject matter than by author's name."

In the periodical section I have noted reprints only where a change of title is involved, in order to avoid cumbersome and sometimes confusing cross-referencing. The reader, if he wishes, may consult the index of titles for the various places a particular essay or story was reprinted.

Unauthorized editions, such as the Russian, and, notably, the pirated Taiwanese editions, are not included simply because I had neither the time nor the resources to track them down.

Many persons have been helpful to me. I would like to thank Miss McCarthy's publishers, both here and abroad; the staff of the UCLA Research Library (with special mention for Mrs. Ann Hinckley, Mr. Richard O'Brien, and Mr. Shimeon Brisman); Miss Dorothy A. Plum, the Vassar College Bibliographer; Miss Frances Goudy, the Vassar Special Collections Librarian; Bishop James P. Shannon of Minneapolis; the Reverend Terrance W. Berntson of the Saint Paul Chancery; Professor Milton Crane of The George Washington University; Mr. Charles Schlessiger of Brandt and Brandt; Mr. Roy Bergquist; and, from the Department of English at UCLA, Professors Hugh Dick, Earl Miner, and Blake Nevius, and, finally, Charles Gullans, who introduced me to and has been my guide through the labyrinthine ways of bibliography.

I would like to thank also my husband, Erwin Goldman, for his encouragement and unflinching editorial eye, and for leading me to the works of Mary McCarthy in the first place.

And, last, I must thank Miss McCarthy herself, who has been more collaborator than subject, and without whose kindness and help this bibliography would be far less complete than it is.

S. E. G.

Los Angeles, California

A

BOOKS

BY

MARY McCARTHY

A. Books

A1 THE COMPANY SHE KEEPS 1942

a. First edition:

THE COMPANY SHE KEEPS | by MARY McCARTHY | SIMON AND SCHUSTER · 1942 [*printed in black in center of olive green panel with pattern of wire screening in white line, top and bottom*] [New York]

x, 304 pp., 1 leaf, 2 blank leaves. 19¾ × 14 cm. $2.50. Gray cloth lettered in black, with black paper label on spine printed in white; end-papers. Gray dust-jacket lettered in yellow and white, with photograph of author on back.

The number of copies printed and the number of printings is unknown because the file on the book was destroyed in a warehouse fire in the 1950's.

CONTENTS: Foreword—Cruel and Barbarous Treatment—Rogue's Gallery—The Man in the Brooks Brothers Shirt—The Genial Host—Portrait of the Intellectual as a Yale Man—Ghostly Father, I Confess.

**b. First English edition:*

THE COMPANY SHE KEEPS . . . London, Weidenfeld and Nicolson, 1943

239 pp. 19 × 12¾ cm. 8s. 6d.

Published in November, 1943.

c. Paperback edition:

THE | COMPANY | SHE | KEEPS | MARY McCARTHY | A DELL BOOK [New York] [1955]

9–223 pp. 16 × 10½ cm. $0.50. White paper lettered in black and red, with a charcoal sketch of lovers embracing on the front cover; edges turquoise.

First published in January, 1955. There have been six subsequent printings, the latest in June, 1965.

d. Second edition:

MARY McCARTHY THE | COMPANY SHE KEEPS | HARCOURT, BRACE AND COMPANY, NEW YORK [1960]

1 blank leaf, 5 leaves, 3–304 pp., 3 blank leaves. 20 × 13 cm. $4.50. Green cloth with design in blind on front and back cov-

ers, lettered in gold downward on spine; end-papers. Green dust-jacket with design in white, yellow, and red, lettered in green, white, and yellow, with photograph of author on back.
Published on August 10, 1960.
CONTENTS: Cruel and Barbarous Treatment—Rogue's Gallery—The Man in the Brooks Brothers Shirt—The Genial Host—Portrait of the Intellectual as a Yale Man—Ghostly Father, I Confess.

**e. Second English edition:*

THE COMPANY SHE KEEPS . . . London, Weidenfeld and Nicolson, 1957

viii, 246 pp., 1 blank leaf. 19 × 12¾ cm. 15s.
3,000 copies were published on June 21, 1957.

**f. English paperback edition:*

THE COMPANY SHE KEEPS . . . London, Penguin Books Ltd., 1965

224 pp. 18 × 12 cm. 4s.
30,000 copies were published on August 26, 1965, with a second printing of 32,000 copies.

A2 THE OASIS 1949

a. First edition:

Mary McCarthy | THE OASIS | [*publisher's device*] | RANDOM HOUSE | New York [1949]

4 leaves, 3–181 pp., 1 blank leaf. 20¼ × 13¼ cm. $2.00. Black cloth lettered downward in gold on spine; end-papers. Red and black dust-jacket lettered in white, with photograph of the author on back.
3,500 copies were published on August 11, 1949. There was a second printing of 1,500 copies on October 6, 1949.
This first appeared in *Horizon* (February, 1949).

**b. First English edition (1950):*

A SOURCE OF EMBARRASSMENT . . . London, William Heinemann Ltd., 1950

vi pp., 1 leaf, 3–193 pp. 18 × 12 cm. 7s. 6d.
3,000 copies were published on May 30, 1950.
(Published in the United States as *The Oasis.*)

**c. English paperback edition:*

A SOURCE OF EMBARRASSMENT . . . London, Panther Books Ltd., 1964

7–127 pp. 17½ × 11 cm. 3s. 6d.
24,000 copies were published in July, 1964, with one subsequent printing (with a different cover design) of 15,000 copies.

A3 CAST A COLD EYE 1950

a. First edition:

MARY McCARTHY | CAST | A COLD EYE | NEW YORK | HARCOURT, BRACE AND COMPANY [1950]

6 leaves, 3–212 pp., 1 blank leaf. 20 × 13¼ cm. $2.75 (current price $3.95). Bright blue cloth lettered in silver on front cover and downward on spine; end-papers. Light blue dust-jacket lettered in navy blue and white, with photograph of the author on back.

Published on September 21, 1950. *On verso of title-page:* first edition. There has been one additional printing.

CONTENTS: The Weeds—The Friend of the Family—The Cicerone—The Old Men—Yonder Peasant, Who Is He?—The Blackguard—C.Y.E.

**b. First English edition:*

CAST A COLD EYE . . . London, William Heinemann Ltd., 1952

4 leaves, 169 pp. 18 × 12 cm. 9s. 6d.
3,000 copies were published on January 14, 1952.

c. Paperback edition:

MARY McCARTHY | CAST A COLD EYE | A SIGNET BOOK PUBLISHED BY | THE NEW AMERICAN LIBRARY | [*publisher's device*] [1963]

212 pp., 2 leaves. 17¾ × 10¼ cm. $0.75. Gray paper with red, lavender, and purple trim, lettered in black, white, and blue, with a sketch of the author on front cover; edges red.

More than 162,000 copies have been published in three printings: two in September, 1963, one in October, 1963. (This edition also contains *The Oasis.*)

A4 THE GROVES OF ACADEME 1952

a. First edition:

Mary McCarthy | THE GROVES | OF ACADEME | New York | HARCOURT, BRACE AND COMPANY [1952]

1 blank leaf, 6 leaves, [3]–302 pp., 3 blank leaves. 20¼ × 13¼ cm. $3.50 (current price $4.50). Light blue cloth with decoration in silver on front cover and lettered downward in silver on spine; end-papers. Orange, blue, and tan dust-jacket depicting surrealistic college scene on front cover, lettered in black, gray, and orange, with photograph of the author on back.

Published on February 21, 1952, with three subsequent printings.

**b. First English edition:*

THE GROVES OF ACADEME . . . London, William Heinemann Ltd., 1953

viii, 1–272 pp. 18 × 12 cm. 12s. 6d.

2,000 copies were published on March 9, 1953, with a second printing of 2,000 copies.

c. Paperback edition:

Mary McCarthy | THE | GROVES | OF | ACADEME | A SIGNET | BOOK [*publisher's device*] | Published by The New American Library [New York] [1963]

255 pp. 17¾ × 10¼ cm. $0.75. White paper with orange, red, and black trim lettered in black, white, and blue; edges red.

About 200,000 copies have been published in three printings: two in October, 1963, one in November, 1963.

**d. English paperback edition:*

THE GROVES OF ACADEME . . . London, Panther Books Ltd., 1964

7–223 pp. 17½ × 11 cm. 3s. 6d.
24,000 copies were published in July, 1964, with one subsequent printing (with a different cover design) of 15,000 copies.

A5 A CHARMED LIFE 1955

a. First edition:

A | Charmed | Life | BY MARY McCARTHY | HARCOURT, BRACE AND COMPANY | NEW YORK [1955]

4 leaves, 3–313 pp. 20 × 13 cm. $3.95. Three-quarter blue paper pasted over yellow cloth on front and back covers, lettered in blue on spine; end-papers. Gray, blue, and yellow dust-jacket depicting surrealistic seacoast scene on front, lettered in black, white, and blue, with photograph of the author on back.
Published on November 3, 1955. *On verso of title-page:* first edition. There have been two subsequent printings.

**b. First English edition:*

A CHARMED LIFE . . . London, Weidenfeld and Nicolson, 1956

3 leaves, 335 pp., 3 blank leaves. 19 × 12¾ cm. 15s.
5,000 copies were published on April 20, 1956.

**c. First paperback edition:*

A CHARMED LIFE . . . New York, Dell Publishing Co., Inc., January, 1958

**d. First English paperback edition:*

A CHARMED LIFE . . . Ace Books, 1961

3s. 6d.
Published February 24, 1961.
(This information is from the *British Catalogue of Books.*)

**e. Second English paperback edition:*

A CHARMED LIFE . . . London, Penguin Books Ltd., 1964

262 pp. 18 × 12 cm. 4s. 6d.
30,000 copies were published on September 24, 1964. 75,000 additional copies have been printed in subsequent printings.

f. Second American paperback edition:

MARY McCARTHY | A CHARMED | LIFE | [*publisher's device*] | A SIGNET BOOK PUBLISHED BY | THE NEW AMERICAN LIBRARY [New York] [1964]

5–223 pp. 17¾ × 10 cm. $0.75. Multicolored paper with needlepoint motif on front cover, lettered in black, white, and red.
215,000 copies were published in February, 1964.

A6 SIGHTS AND SPECTACLES 1937–1956 1956

a. First edition:

Mary McCarthy | Sights and | Spectacles | 1937–1956 | FARRAR, STRAUS AND CUDAHY • New York [1956]

xvi, 3–183 pp. 20¾ × 13¼ cm. $3.50. Vermilion cloth lettered in black on spine as follows: [*downward*] Mary McCarthy Sights and Spectacles, [*across*] Farrar | Straus | And | Cudahy; endpapers; top edges gray. White dust-jacket lettered in black, white, and red, with photograph of author on front.
Published on May 25, 1956. *On verso of title-page:* First printing, 1956.
CONTENTS: Introduction—Two Bad Cases of Social Conscience—Odets Deplored—Elizabethan Revivals—Class Angles and a Wilder Classic—The Federal Theatre—Shaw and Chekhov—Saroyan, An Innocent on Broadway—The Skin of Our Teeth—The Russian Soul in Wartime—Broadway's Spring Offensive—Wartime Omnibus—We Must Have Faith—Eugene O'Neill—Dry Ice—Five Curios—George Kelly—The Unimportance of Being Oscar—Three Plays with Music—What a Piece of Work Is Man!—Four "Well-Made" Plays—A Streetcar Called Success—Little Theatre—A Prince of Shreds and Patches—The Little Gate—Shaw Off Broadway—The Family Tea Party—The Will and Testament of Ibsen.

**b. First English edition:*

SIGHTS AND SPECTACLES . . . London, William Heinemann Ltd., 1959

xxv, 1–202 pp. 21 × 14 cm. 18s.
6,000 copies were published on March 2, 1959.

**c. Paperback edition:*

Sights and Spectacles . . . New York, Meridian Books, February, 1957

183 pp. $1.25.

A7 VENICE OBSERVED 1956

a. First edition:

VENICE | OBSERVED | By Mary McCarthy | G. & R. Bernier Paris Lausanne | Reynal & Company New York [1956]

[5]–199 pp. 30¼ × 23½ cm. Illustrated. $15.00. Paper boards with four-color photographic reproduction of painting detail with acetate-laminate overlay, lettered in white on front cover and stamped, downward, in gold on white simulated leather spine. The dust-jacket duplicates the front and back covers, with the same acetate-laminate overlay, lettered in white on front and in black on spine.

According to the publisher, there was one printing of 15,000 copies in November, 1956. *On verso of last page:* First printing: September 15, 1956–Second edition: March 15, 1957.

**b. First English edition:*

VENICE OBSERVED . . . London, A. Zwemmer Ltd., 1956

200 pp. 31¼ × 25¼ cm. 90s.
Published in November, 1956.

**c. Second English edition:*

VENICE OBSERVED . . . London, William Heinemann Ltd., 1961

1 leaf, vi, 158 pp., 1 blank leaf. 18 × 12 cm. 15s.
2,500 copies were published on November 27, 1961.

d. Paperback edition:

Mary McCarthy | Venice Observed | [*publisher's device*] | A Harvest Book | Harcourt, Brace & World, Inc. [*line*] New York [1963]

4 leaves, [1]–158 pp., 1 blank leaf. 18¼ × 10¾ cm. $1.35. Blue and white paper with architectural detail in orange and gold on front cover, lettered in blue, white, and gold.

Published on September 25, 1963, with two subsequent printings.

A8 MEMORIES OF A CATHOLIC GIRLHOOD 1957

a. First edition:

Mary McCarthy | MEMORIES OF A | CATHOLIC GIRLHOOD | [*floral ornament in mauve*] | Harcourt, Brace and Company • New York [1957]

6 leaves, [3]–245 pp., 8 pages of photographs between pp. 86 and [87]. 20 × 13¼ cm. $3.95 (current price $4.75). Black cloth with ivory paper label on spine in facsimile of author's handwriting in purple; end-papers. Purple dust-jacket with white floral design, lettered in white, with photograph of the author's family on back.

First published on May 16, 1957. *On verso of title-page:* first edition. There have been three subsequent printings.

CONTENTS: To the Reader—Yonder Peasant, Who Is He?—A Tin Butterfly—The Blackguard—*C'est le Premier Pas Qui Coûte*—Names—The Figures in the Clock—Yellowstone Park—Ask Me No Questions.

**b. First English edition:*

MEMORIES OF A CATHOLIC GIRLHOOD . . . London, William Heinemann Ltd., 1957

xxxiv, 1–260 pp., 8 pages of photographs between pp. 30 and 31. 21 × 14 cm. 21s.

6,000 copies were published on November 18, 1957.

c. Paperback edition:

MEMORIES | OF A | CATHOLIC | GIRLHOOD | Mary McCarthy | [*publisher's device*] | A BERKLEY MEDALLION BOOK | published by | BERKLEY PUBLISHING CORPORATION [1963]

9–224 pp. 17¾ × 10¼ cm. $0.60. Green paper with yellow and red butterfly ornament, lettered in black, white, and yellow; edges red.

77,400 copies were published in October, 1963. There have been three subsequent printings: November, 1963, August, 1964, and February, 1966, with 25,968, 77,629, and 25,681 copies in each, respectively.

**d. English paperback edition:*

MEMORIES OF A CATHOLIC GIRLHOOD . . . London, Penguin Books Ltd., 1963

18 × 10½ cm. 3s. 6d.
52,000 copies were published on February 21, 1963.

A9 THE STONES OF FLORENCE 1959

**a. First English edition:*

THE STONES OF FLORENCE . . . London, William Heinemann Ltd., 1959

228 pp. Illustrated. 28½ × 22½ cm. 84s.
4,200 copies were published on October 19, 1959.

b. First American edition:

THE STONES OF | FLORENCE | BY MARY McCARTHY | PHOTOGRAPHS BY EVELYN HOFER AND OTHERS | NEW YORK [*ornament*] HARCOURT, BRACE AND COMPANY [1959]

1 leaf, [iii], frontispiece, [v–xi], one plate between each leaf pp. 3–26, two plates, 27–28, two plates, 29–30, plate, 31–32, two plates, 33–36, two plates, 37–38, two plates, 39–49, two plates, one plate between each leaf pp. 41–64, two plates, one plate between each leaf pp. 65–74, two plates, one plate between each leaf pp. 75–82, two plates, one plate between each leaf pp. 83–94, two plates, one plate between each leaf pp. 95–100, two plates, 101–102, one plate between each leaf pp. 103–108, two plates, 109–110, plate, 111–114, two plates, 115–118, plate, 119, [120], 121–130 pp. 27½ × 21 cm. $15.00 (current price $17.50). Saffron cloth lettered downward in gold on spine; black end-papers. Black and white dust-jacket with photographic detail on front, lettered in black, white, and gold.

First published on October 21, 1959, with four subsequent printings. *On verso of title-page:* Some of the text in this book originally appeared, in different form, in *The New Yorker.*

c. Paperback edition:

Mary McCarthy | The Stones of Florence | [*publisher's device*] | A Harvest Book | Harcourt, Brace & World, Inc. [*line*] New York [1963]

4 leaves, 1–230 pp., 1 blank leaf. 18¼ × 10½ cm. $1.35. Black and white paper with architectural detail on front cover, lettered in black, white, and saffron.

Published on September 25, 1963, with three subsequent printings.

**d. Unillustrated English edition:*

THE STONES OF FLORENCE . . . London, William Heinemann Ltd., 1963

viii, 1–230 pp., 1 blank leaf. 18 × 12 cm. 18s.

1,750 copies were published on June 17, 1963.

A10 ON THE CONTRARY 1961

a. First edition:

ON | THE | CONTRARY | MARY McCARTHY | FARRAR, STRAUS | AND CUDAHY | NEW YORK [1961]

vii–[viii] pp., 1 leaf, 312 pp. 20 × 13¼ cm. $4.50. Gray cloth lettered downward in white, red, and black on spine; end-papers; top edges red. White dust-jacket lettered in red and black, with photograph of the author on front.

Published on September 26, 1961. There has been one subsequent printing.

CONTENTS: A Letter to the Editor of *Politics*—America the Beautiful: The Humanist in the Bathtub—Gandhi—*Mlle. Gulliver en Amérique*—No News, *or,* What Killed the Dog—The Contagion of Ideas—Artists in Uniform—My Confession—Letter From Portugal—Mister Rodriguez of Lisbon—Naming Names: The Arthur Miller Case—The *Vita Activa*—Tyranny of the Orgasm—Up the Ladder from *Charm* to *Vogue*—The Vassar

Girl—Recalled to Life, *or,* Charles Dickens at the Bar—Settling the Colonel's Hash—An Academy of Risk—The Fact in Fiction —Characters in Fiction—The American Realist Playwrights.

b. Paperback edition:

ON | THE | CONTRARY | MARY | McCARTHY | NOONDAY PRESS | *a division of* | FARRAR, STRAUS | AND COMPANY | NEW YORK [1961]

[i]–vii, [viii], 1 leaf, 3–312 pp. 20 × 13¼ cm. $1.95. White paper lettered in red and black, with photograph of the author on front cover.

Published on September 26, 1961. There have been three subsequent printings.

**c. First English edition:*

ON THE CONTRARY . . . London, William Heinemann Ltd., 1962

3 leaves, 1–312 pp., 1 blank leaf. 20 × 13 cm. 30s.

1,500 copies were published on July 23, 1962, with a second printing of 1,000 copies.

A11 MARY McCARTHY'S THEATRE CHRONICLES 1937–1962 1963

a. First edition:

Mary McCarthy's | Theatre Chronicles 1937–1962 | BY MARY McCARTHY | FARRAR, STRAUS AND COMPANY | New York [1963]

xxi, [xxii], 1 leaf, 3–248 pp., 1 blank leaf. 20¼ × 13½ cm. $4.50. Blue cloth lettered downward in silver on spine; end-papers; top edges dark blue. Light blue and black dust-jacket lettered in white, with author's photograph on front.

Published on August 15, 1963. There has been one subsequent printing.

CONTENTS: All of the pieces in *Sights and Spectacles,* with the following additional chapters: Introduction—Sheep in Wolves' Clothing—A New Word—Odd Man In—Drapes—General Macbeth.

b. Paperback edition:

Mary McCarthy's | Theatre Chronicles 1937–1962 | BY MARY McCARTHY | THE NOONDAY PRESS | *a division of* | FARRAR, STRAUS AND COMPANY | New York [1963]

xxi, [xxii], 1 leaf, 3–248 pp., 1 blank leaf. 20¼ × 13½ cm. $1.95. Light blue, black, and white paper, lettered in white and black, with author's photograph on front cover.

Published on August 15, 1963.

A12 THE GROUP 1963

a. First edition:

THE GROUP | BY MARY McCARTHY | NEW YORK | HARCOURT, BRACE & WORLD, INC. [1963]

3 leaves, 3–378 pp., 1 blank leaf. 21 × 14 cm. $5.95. Periwinkle blue cloth lettered in silver on spine as follows: [*across*] Mary | McCarthy, [*downward*] The Group, [*across*] Harcourt, | Brace | & World; end-papers. White and gray dust-jacket with daisy motif on front cover and on spine, lettered in shades of pink, blue, and combinations of the two, with photograph of the author on back.

First published on August 28, 1963. *On verso of title-page:* first edition. There have been six subsequent printings.

**b. First English edition:*

THE GROUP . . . London, Weidenfeld and Nicolson Ltd., 1963

360 pp. 20¼ × 13½ cm. 18s.

25,000 copies were published in October, 1963. There have been twelve subsequent printings totaling 100,000 copies.

c. Paperback edition:

THE | GROUP | Mary McCarthy | A SIGNET BOOK | Published by THE NEW AMERICAN LIBRARY | [*publisher's device*] [New York] [1964]

7–397 pp., 1 leaf. 17½ × 10¼ cm. $0.95. White and gray paper with daisy motif on front cover, lettered in black, gray, and shades of red and blue; edges red.

There have been sixteen printings: five in September, 1964, one in November, 1964, one in November, 1965, two in February, 1966, four in May, 1966, two in August, 1966, and one in October, 1966, totaling over 2,600,000 copies.

**d. English paperback edition:*

THE GROUP . . . London, Penguin Books Ltd., 1965

349 pp. 18 × 12 cm. 6s.
40,000 copies were published in 1965.

A13 THE HUMANIST IN THE BATHTUB 1964

Paperback edition:

MARY McCARTHY | The Humanist | in the Bathtub | Selected Essays from Mary McCarthys' [*sic*] | Theatre Chronicles 1937–1962 | and On the Contrary | A SIGNET BOOK published by | THE NEW AMERICAN LIBRARY | [*publisher's device*] [New York] [1964]

7–216 pp. 17½ × 10¼ cm. $0.75. Gray and white paper trimmed in red, black, and orange, lettered in red, white, and black, with photograph of the author on front cover.
160,000 copies were published in June, 1964.
CONTENTS: America the Beautiful: The Humanist in the Bathtub—*Mlle. Gulliver en Amérique*—The American Realist Playwrights—The Vassar Girl—Artists in Uniform—Settling the Colonel's Hash—A New Word—Odd Man In—Drapes—My Confession—Tyranny of the Orgasm—An Academy of Risk—The Fact in Fiction—Characters in Fiction.

A14 VIETNAM 1967

First edition:

Mary McCarthy | VIETNAM | HARCOURT, BRACE & WORLD, INC., NEW YORK [1967] | [*publisher's device*]

6 leaves, 3–106 pp., 2 blank leaves. 22¾ × 15 cm. $1.95. Latex-coated textured paper with design in black, white, red, and

green, lettered in black, white, and green, with a photograph of Miss McCarthy on the front cover.

Published on September 6, 1967. *On verso of title-page:* First edition. This edition has an erratum slip inserted which reads "The sentence on page 95 beginning on line 2 should read: And what if the bombing stops and Hanoi does not come to the conference table or comes with intransigent terms?"

A reprinting of "Report from Vietnam" in *The New York Review of Books* (April 20, May 4, and May 18, 1967), with an additional chapter, "Solutions."

B

BOOKS WITH CONTRIBUTIONS BY MARY McCARTHY[1]

[1] *Listed chronologically by year, and alphabetically by anthology title within each year.*

B1 "GHOSTLY FATHER, I CONFESS" 1944

It's a | Woman's | World [*device*] | A Collection of | Stories from | HARPER'S BAZAAR | Edited by | MARY LOUISE ASWELL | Whittlesey House | MCGRAW-HILL BOOK COMPANY, INC. | New York --------- London [1944]

x pp., 1 leaf, 346 pp., 1 blank leaf. 22½ × 14½ cm. $3.00. Beige cloth stamped in blue on front cover and on spine; end-papers; top edges blue. Dust-jacket unseen.

Published on April 3, 1944.

Contains "Ghostly Father, I Confess," by Mary McCarthy: pp. 261–300, reprinted from *Harper's Bazaar,* April, 1942.

B2 "CHAOS IS COME AGAIN" AND "THE MAN IN THE BROOKS BROTHERS SHIRT" 1946

[*downward*] THE | PARTISAN | [*downward*] READER | TEN YEARS OF PARTISAN REVIEW | 1934–1944: AN ANTHOLOGY | EDITED BY | WILLIAM PHILLIPS AND PHILIP RAHV | INTRODUCTION BY | LIONEL TRILLING | THE DIAL PRESS, NEW YORK, 1946

xvi pp., 1 leaf, 688 pp. 20¾ × 13½ cm. $3.75. Yellow buckram stamped in black on front cover and on spine; end-papers. Dust-jacket unseen.

Published in 1946.

Contains "The Man in the Brooks Brothers Shirt": pp. 110–141 (reprinted from *Partisan Review,* July–August, 1941), and "Chaos Is Come Again": pp. 655–657 (reprinted from *Partisan Review,* January–February, 1943), by Mary McCarthy.

B3 "PORTRAIT OF THE INTELLECTUAL AS A YALE MAN" 1947

THE | ROOSEVELT | ERA | Edited by | Milton Crane | With a Foreword by | Jonathan Daniels | [*device*] | Boni and Gaer New York [1947] xiv pp., 1 leaf, 626 pp. 20 × 13 cm. $4.75 (Standard edition) and $10.00 (Limited edition). Blue cloth stamped in gold (Standard), blue with quarter red cloth stamped in silver (Limited); end-papers. Dust-jacket with sketch of burning cigarette in a holder lying across a document bearing the presidential seal.

Published in Fall, 1947.

Contains "Portrait of the Intellectual as a Yale Man," by Mary McCarthy: pp. 253–301.

B4 "AMERICA THE BEAUTIFUL: THE HUMANIST IN THE BATHTUB" 1948

NEW | DIRECTIONS | 10 | in prose and poetry | AN ANNUAL EXHIBITION GALLERY OF NEW | AND DIVERGENT TRENDS IN LITERATURE | [Parsippany, New Jersey, Blue Ridge Mountain Press: 1948]

512 pp. 22¾ × 15 cm. $4.50. Gray buckram stamped in red on spine; end-papers.

Edited by James Laughlin; published in 1948.

Contains "America the Beautiful: The Humanist in the Bathtub," by Mary McCarthy: pp. 23–33, reprinted from *Commentary*, September, 1947.

B5 "YONDER PEASANT, WHO IS HE?" 1949

55 SHORT STORIES | FROM | THE | NEW YORKER | [New Yorker *emblem*] | SIMON AND SCHUSTER · NEW YORK [1949]

viii pp., 1 leaf, 480 pp. 22½ × 14½ cm. $4.00.

Contains "Yonder Peasant, Who Is He?" by Mary McCarthy: pp. 172–184, reprinted from *The New Yorker*, December 4, 1948.

*B6 "THE UNSPOILED REACTION" 1950

Patterns in Writing . . . New York, William Sloane Associates, Inc., 1950 xi, 702 pp. $3.00.

Reprinted by Holt, Rinehart and Winston on March 8, 1963. Turquoise and dark green cloth stamped in turquoise; end-papers. No dust-jacket.

Edited by Robert Barnard Doremus and others.

Contains "The Unspoiled Reaction," by Mary McCarthy: pp. 627–635.

B7 "SOMETHING ABOUT THE WEATHER" 1953

[Partisan Review *device*] | THE NEW PARTISAN READER | 1945–1953 | EDITED BY | William Phillips | AND | Philip Rahv | HARCOURT, BRACE AND COMPANY [*publisher's device*] NEW YORK [1953]

xii, 621 pp., 2 blank leaves. 20¼ × 13½ cm. $6.00 (later price $6.75). Light blue buckram stamped in black on front cover and downward on spine; end-papers.

Published on October 22, 1953. *On verso of title-page:* first edition.

Contains "Something About the Weather," by Mary McCarthy: pp. 531–536, reprinted from *Partisan Review,* March–April, 1947.

B8 "CRUEL AND BARBAROUS TREATMENT" 1953

[*five line bar*] | An Anthology of | STORIES | from the | SOUTHERN REVIEW | Edited by | CLEANTH BROOKS | and | ROBERT PENN WARREN | LOUISIANA STATE UNIVERSITY PRESS | Baton Rouge | [*five line bar*] [1953]

xvi, 435 pp. 22½ × 15 cm. $6.00. Green buckram stamped in black and gold on spine; end-papers; top edges yellow.

2,500 copies were published in November, 1953.

Contains "Cruel and Barbarous Treatment," by Mary McCarthy: pp. 249–261, reprinted from *The Southern Review,* Spring, 1939.

B9 "THE UNSPOILED REACTION" 1954

Contemporary Short Stories | Representative Selections | Edited, with an Introduction, by | MAURICE BAUDIN, JR. | Assistant Professor of English | New York University | VOLUME THREE | THE LIBERAL ARTS PRESS | NEW YORK [1954]

ix, 237 pp. 20¼ × 13½ cm. $6.50 (for the three-volume set). Green cloth stamped in red and gold on front cover, and on spine as follows: [*downward*] CONTEMPORARY | SHORT STORIES III, [*across*] M. BAUDIN | Ed. | THE | LIBERAL | ARTS | PRESS; end-papers; top edges green.

Published in 1954.

Contains "The Unspoiled Reaction," by Mary McCarthy: pp. 214–224, reprinted from *The Atlantic Monthly,* March, 1946.

B10 "THE GROUP" 1954

AVON BOOK OF | MODERN WRITING | No. 2 | edited by William Phillips | & Philip Rahv | An entirely new collection of hitherto | unpublished fiction, poetry, etc. by | Eric Bentley | Benjamin DeMott | Horace Gregory | Elizabeth Hardwick | Hermann Hesse | Mary McCarthy | Alberto Moravia | V. S. Pritchett | Delmore Schwartz | And 18 others [Avon Publications, Inc., New York] [1954]

9–318 pp., 1 leaf. 17¼ × 10¼ cm. $0.50. Multicolored paper lettered in black and red.

Published in 1954. *On verso of title-page:* Copyright, 1954, by Avon Publications, Inc. . . .

Contains "The Group," by Mary McCarthy: pp. 32–54. (Reprinted in revised form as Chapter 1 of *The Group.*)

B11 "THE CICERONE" 1954

MORE STORIES IN THE [*on the left of a double page opening; the rest is* en face:] MODERN MANNER | From Partisan Review | James Agee | Benjamin DeMott | Angus Wilson | Marcel Proust | Franz Kafka | Lionel Trilling | Isaac Bashevis Singer | Alberto Moravia | Elisabeth Langgässer | Paul Goodman | Jean

Stafford | Mary McCarthy | Elizabeth Hardwick | Saul Bellow | AVON PUBLICATIONS, INC. | 575 Madison Avenue • New York 22, N.Y. [1954]

252 pp. 17½ × 10½ cm. $0.50. Paperback.
Published in 1954.
Contains "The Cicerone," by Mary McCarthy: pp. 64–90, reprinted from *Partisan Review,* February, 1948.

B12 "ARTISTS IN UNIFORM" AND "SETTLING THE COLONEL'S HASH" 1955

[*to right of broken line in center of page:*] CONTRASTS | [*left of line:*] IDEA | AND TECHNIQUE | [*right:*] Edited by Robert E. Knoll | University of Nebraska | [*left:*] Harcourt, Brace and Company | New York [1955]

575 pp. 21½ × 14 cm. $3.75 (later price $4.00). Tan cloth and dark blue latex-coated paper lettered in black; end-papers. No dust-jacket.
First published on January 13, 1955, with four subsequent printings.
Contains "Artists in Uniform": pp. 370–383, and "Settling the Colonel's Hash": pp. 383–394, both by Mary McCarthy.

B13 "SETTLING THE COLONEL'S HASH" 1955

ESSAYS TODAY | Editor, RICHARD M. LUDWIG | PRINCETON UNIVERSITY | NEW YORK [*short vertical line*] HARCOURT, BRACE AND COMPANY [1955]

vi, 181 pp. 20½ × 13½ cm. $2.50. Blue and brown paper lettered in white and blue.
Published on May 3, 1955.
Contains "Settling the Colonel's Hash," by Mary McCarthy: pp. 84–94, reprinted from *Harper's Magazine,* February, 1954.

B14 "ARTISTS IN UNIFORM" 1955
AND
"SETTLING
THE COLONEL'S HASH"

[*title only enclosed in decorative border*] Patterns for Living | EDITED BY | OSCAR JAMES CAMPBELL | *Columbia University* | JUSTINE VAN GUNDY | *San Francisco State College* | CAROLINE SHRODES | *San Francisco State College* | FOURTH EDITION | *New York* | THE MACMILLAN COMPANY [1955]

v–[xvi] pp., 1 leaf, 975 pp. 23¼ × 15½ cm. $5.00. Medium green buckram stamped in dark green and silver on front cover and on spine; end-papers. No dust-jacket.

17,000 copies were published on March 22, 1955. There have been five subsequent printings, totaling over 30,000 copies.

Contains "Artists in Uniform": pp. 606–617, and "Settling the Colonel's Hash": pp. 617–628, both by Mary McCarthy.

*B15 "CRUEL AND 1955
BARBAROUS TREATMENT"

This Thing Called Love. New York, New American Library of World Literature, Inc., 1955

143 pp. $0.25.

A Signet Book edited by Marc Slonim and Harvey Breit.

Contains "Cruel and Barbarous Treatment," by Mary McCarthy.

B16 "DOTTIE MAKES AN 1956
HONEST WOMAN OF HERSELF"

DAUGHTERS | OF EVE | A collection of stories by | WILLIAM FAULKNER | ALBERTO MORAVIA | D. H. LAWRENCE | JOHN STEINBECK | W. SOMERSET MAUGHAM | H. E. BATES | MARY McCARTHY | JOHN COLLIER | JOHN CHEEVER | [*publisher's device*] | A BERKLEY MEDALLION BOOK | published by | BERKLEY PUBLISHING CORPORATION [1956]

192 pp. 17¾ × 10½ cm. $0.35 (first printing) and $0.50 (second printing). Multicolored paper, lettered in yellow, white, black, and red, with photographic portrait on front cover; edges red.

110,000 copies were published in November, 1956, with an additional printing of 70,000 copies in April, 1962.

Contains "Dottie Makes an Honest Woman of Herself," by Mary McCarthy: pp. 172–192, reprinted from *Partisan Review,* January–February, 1954. (Reprinted, in revised form, as Chapter 3 of *The Group.*)

B17 "UP THE LADDER FROM CHARM TO VOGUE" 1956

THE | REPORTER | READER | EDITED BY MAX ASCOLI | EDITOR OF THE REPORTER | A Fortnightly of Facts and Ideas | Doubleday & Company, Inc., 1956 | Garden City, N.Y.

3 leaves, 1–314 pp. 17¼ × 10 cm. $1.00. Black, green, blue, and white paper, lettered in black and white, with world globe design on front cover.

37,500 copies were published on January 10, 1956. *On verso of title-page:* First Edition.

Contains "Up the Ladder From *Charm* to *Vogue,*" by Mary McCarthy: pp. 152–168.

B18 "YELLOWSTONE PARK" 1957

PRIZE STORIES | 1957 | THE O. HENRY AWARDS | Selected and Edited by PAUL ENGLE | Assisted by CONSTANCE URDANG | DOUBLEDAY & COMPANY, INC., GARDEN CITY, NEW YORK, 1957

1 leaf, [5]–312 pp. 20¾ × 13¾ cm. $3.95. Black buckram stamped in white on spine; end-papers; top edges green. Black, white, blue, and pink dust-jacket lettered in black, white, and pink.

8,500 copies were published on January 10, 1957. *On verso of title-page:* First Edition.

Contains "Yellowstone Park," by Mary McCarthy: pp. 292–309, reprinted from *Harper's Bazaar,* November, 1955.

B19 "AMERICA THE BEAUTIFUL" 1958

THE | ART | OF THE | ESSAY | EDITED, WITH INTRODUCTIONS, NOTES | AND EXERCISE QUESTIONS BY | LESLIE FIEDLER | MONTANA STATE UNIVERSITY | THOMAS Y. CROWELL COMPANY | NEW YORK [1958]

1 leaf, v–xvii, 1–640 pp., 2 blank leaves. 22½ × 15 cm. $6.00 ($4.25 in the text edition). Two-tone green buckram stamped in black and cream on front cover and on spine; end-papers. No dust-jacket.

5,000 copies were published on March 28, 1958. There was an additional printing of 10,000 copies in 1958, and a third printing of 2,500 copies in 1963.

Contains "America the Beautiful," by Mary McCarthy: pp. 247–256.

B20 "LIFE AT 'JOCELYN COLLEGE'" 1958

Education in Society: | Readings | BERNARD N. MELTZER | HARRY R. DOBY | PHILIP M. SMITH | THOMAS Y. CROWELL COMPANY, NEW YORK [1958]

xiv, 498 pp. 21 × 13½ cm. $3.75. Gray cloth lettered in red and white on front cover and on spine; end-papers. Dust-jacket unseen.

7,500 copies were published on March 6, 1958. 3,000 additional copies were printed in a later impression.

Contains "Life at 'Jocelyn College,'" by Mary McCarthy: pp. 74–76, reprinted from *The Groves of Academe.*

B21 "CRUEL AND BARBAROUS TREATMENT" 1959

CLEANTH BROOKS | ROBERT PENN WARREN | Understanding FICTION | SECOND EDITION | [*publisher's device*] | NEW YORK | Appleton-Century-Crofts, Inc. [1959]

xxiii, 1–688 pp. 23¼ × 15¼ cm. $5.50. Brown buckram stamped in white on front cover, and on spine as follows: [*across*]

BROOKS | & | WARREN | [*downward*] Understanding FICTION | [*across*] APPLETON | CENTURY | CROFTS; end-papers.

Published in 1959.

Contains "Cruel and Barbarous Treatment," by Mary McCarthy: pp. 251–261.

B22 "GRANDMOTHER" 1959

[*double page opening;* en face:] THE DEPARTMENT OF ENGLISH | WAYNE STATE UNIVERSITY | [*on left:*] WRITING | [en face:] FROM OBSERVATION | REVISED | *under the editorship of* | LESTER W. CAMERON | SAMUEL A. GOLDEN [*on left:*] THIRD EDITION | [en face:] [*publisher's device*] *Harcourt, Brace and Company* | *New York* [1959]

vii–xvi pp., 2 leaves, 3–523 pp., 1 leaf. 21¼ × 14 cm. $3.75 (later price $4.50). Latex-coated paper with needlepoint design in gray on white on front cover, with colors reversed on back cover; lettered in turquoise on front cover and downward in black and white on turquoise spine; end-papers. No dust-jacket.

Published on January 30, 1959, with two subsequent printings.

Contains "Grandmother," by Mary McCarthy: pp. 94–101, a reprinting of "Ask Me No Questions."

B23 "SETTLING THE COLONEL'S HASH" 1960

WALTER B. RIDEOUT | NORTHWESTERN UNIVERSITY | The | Experience | of Prose | THOMAS Y. CROWELL COMPANY | NEW YORK *Established* 1834 [1960]

v–xvi, 1–624 pp. 22½ × 14½ cm. $4.50 ($2.95 in paperback). Dark blue cloth stamped in white on front cover and in white and green on spine; end-papers. Mustard and beige dust-jacket.

7,500 copies were published on January 4, 1960.

Contains "Settling the Colonel's Hash," by Mary McCarthy: pp. 151–162.

B24 "SETTLING THE COLONEL'S HASH" 1960

LITERARY SYMBOLISM | An Introduction | to the | Interpretation | of Literature | edited by Maurice Beebe | Purdue University | WADSWORTH PUBLISHING COMPANY, INC. | SAN FRANCISCO [1960]

ix pp., 1 leaf, 181 pp. 20½ × 13½ cm. $3.00 ($2.25 in the text edition). Turquoise and white paper, with design in black on front cover, lettered in white, black, and turquoise.

7,500 copies were published on March 19, 1960. There have been four subsequent printings of 7,500, 3,000, 5,500, and 3,000 copies, respectively.

Contains "Settling the Colonel's Hash," by Mary McCarthy: pp. 43–54, reprinted from *Harper's Magazine,* February, 1954.

B25 "THE UNSPOILED REACTION" 1960

JOSHUA McCLENNEN | University of Michigan | [*decorative line*] | Masters | and Masterpieces | of the Short Story | SECOND SERIES | HOLT, RINEHART AND WINSTON · NEW YORK [1960]

viii pp., 1 leaf, 1–562 pp., 2 blank leaves. 20¾ × 13¾ cm. $3.25. Blue paper with ocean photograph on front cover, lettered in white and yellow on front cover and on spine.

First published on February 25, 1960.

Contains "The Unspoiled Reaction," by Mary McCarthy: pp. 425–431.

B26 "ASK ME NO QUESTIONS" 1960

STORIES FROM | THE | NEW YORKER | 1950–1960 | [New Yorker *emblem*] | SIMON AND SCHUSTER · NEW YORK [1960]

3 leaves, v–vii pp., 2 leaves, 1–780 pp., 3 blank leaves. 22¾ × 15 cm. $7.50. Light blue buckram stamped in black on front cover and in black and gold on spine; end-papers.

Published in 1960.

Contains "Ask Me No Questions," by Mary McCarthy: pp. 353–391, reprinted from *The New Yorker,* March, 1957.

B27 "AMERICA THE BEAUTIFUL" 1961

Form | and | Focus | Robert F. McDonnell | William E. Morris | OHIO UNIVERSITY | [*publisher's device*] HARCOURT, BRACE & WORLD, INC. | NEW YORK AND BURLINGAME [1961]

v–ix pp., 1 leaf, 405 pp. 22¾ × 15½ cm. $2.95 (current price $4.25). Black and aqua paper with a geometric design on front and back covers, lettered in aqua, black, and white on front cover and on spine.

First published on April 10, 1961, with seven subsequent printings.

Contains "America the Beautiful," by Mary McCarthy: pp. 312–320.

B28 "A MOON FOR THE MISBEGOTTEN" 1961

O'NEILL | AND HIS PLAYS | FOUR DECADES OF CRITICISM | EDITED BY | Oscar Cargill | N. Bryllion Fagin | William J. Fisher | NEW YORK UNIVERSITY PRESS [*publisher's device*] [1961]

v–[xii] pp., 1 leaf, 528 pp., 1 blank leaf. 23¼ × 15 cm. $7.50. Royal blue buckram with half overlay of olive green buckram, stamped in red and olive green on spine; end-papers. Mauve dust-jacket lettered in black, gray, and white.

Published in 1961. (See also the paperback edition, 1963, listed below.)

Contains "A Moon For The Misbegotten," by Mary McCarthy: pp. 209–211, reprinted from *Sights and Spectacles,* where it appears as "Eugene O'Neill–Dry Ice."

B29 "JOCELYN COLLEGE" 1962

[*woodcut*] | AMERICAN SATIRE | in Prose and Verse | Edited by Henry C. Carlisle, Jr. | [*publisher's device*] | RANDOM HOUSE | NEW YORK [1962]

3 leaves, v–xxiv pp., 2 leaves, 3–464 pp., 1 leaf, 1 blank leaf. 21 × 14¼ cm. $6.95 (current price $7.50). Red cloth stamped in

gold on front cover and in gold and blind on spine; end-papers; top edges blue.

First published on October 3, 1962. There was an additional printing in 1963. *On verso of title-page:* FIRST PRINTING.

Contains "Jocelyn College (from *The Groves of Academe*)," by Mary McCarthy: pp. 248–253.

B30 "MY CONFESSION" 1963

ENCOUNTERS | An Anthology from the First Ten Years | of *Encounter* Magazine | *Editors:* | STEPHEN SPENDER, IRVING KRISTOL, | MELVIN J. LASKY | *Selected by* | MELVIN J. LASKY | BASIC BOOKS, Inc., Publishers | New York [1963]

xiii pp., 1 leaf, [562] pp. 23¼ × 15¼ cm. $8.50. Vermilion cloth stamped in blue and gold on spine as follows: [*downward, in gold*] ENCOUNTERS [*underlined by blue bar design and gold bar*], [*downward, in blue*] *Editors:* STEPHEN SPENDER | IRVING KRISTOL | MELVIN J. LASKY, [*across,* in gold] BASIC BOOKS; end-papers. Red and black dust-jacket lettered in red and white.

Published on October 23, 1963.

Contains "My Confession," by Mary McCarthy: pp. 34–54.

B31 "AMERICA THE BEAUTIFUL" 1963

FIRST | PERSON | SINGULAR | [*bar*] | ESSAYS FOR THE SIXTIES | EDITED AND | WITH AN INTRODUCTION BY | HERBERT GOLD | [*publisher's device*] | THE DIAL PRESS, NEW YORK, 1963

254 pp., 1 blank leaf. 20 × 13½ cm. $5.00. Blue cloth stamped in white on front cover and on spine as follows: [*downward*] FIRST PERSON SINGULAR Herbert Gold | [*across*] [*publisher's device*] | Dial; end-papers. Brown dust-jacket lettered in blue and white.

4,000 copies were published on June 28, 1963.

Contains "America the Beautiful: The Humanist in the Bathtub," by Mary McCarthy: pp. 160–172.

B32 "A TIN BUTTERFLY" 1963

[*double page opening; on left:*] INQUIRY [en face:] AND a college reader | EXPRESSION | [*device*] REVISED EDITION | [*on left:*] HOLT, RINEHART AND WINSTON, INC. | NEW YORK – CHICAGO – SAN FRANCISCO – TORONTO [1963] | [en face:] Harold C. Martin, HARVARD UNIVERSITY | Richard M. Ohmann, WESLEYAN UNIVERSITY

iv–[xvi] pp., 2 leaves, 3–812 pp., 1 blank leaf. 22½ × 15 cm. $6.75. Brown buckram stamped in mustard and silver on front cover and on spine and in silver on back cover; end-papers. No dust-jacket.

First published on March 7, 1963.

Contains "A Tin Butterfly," by Mary McCarthy: pp. 675–682.

B33 "GENERAL MACBETH" 1963

William Shakespeare | The Tragedy of | MACBETH | Edited by Sylvan Barnet | The Signet Classic Shakespeare | GENERAL EDITOR: SYLVAN BARNET | [*publisher's device*] | PUBLISHED BY THE NEW AMERICAN LIBRARY | NEW YORK AND TORONTO | THE NEW ENGLISH LIBRARY LIMITED, LONDON [1963]

xxxiii pp., 1 leaf, 37–[248] pp. 18 × 10¼ cm. $0.50. White paper lettered in black, with illustration on front cover.

Published in 1963.

Contains "General Macbeth," by Mary McCarthy: pp. 229–240, reprinted from *Harper's Magazine,* June, 1962.

B34 "A MOON FOR THE MISBEGOTTEN" 1963

O'NEILL | AND HIS PLAYS | FOUR DECADES OF CRITICISM | EDITED BY | Oscar Cargill | N. Bryllion Fagin | William J. Fisher | NEW YORK UNIVERSITY PRESS [*publisher's device*] [1963]

v–[xii] pp., 1 leaf, 528 pp., 1 blank leaf. 22¾ × 15 cm. $2.95. Black paper with portrait of O'Neill in red on front cover; lettered in white and red on front cover and on spine, and in black on white back cover.

Published in 1963. (See also the hard-cover edition, 1961, listed above.)

Contains "A Moon For The Misbegotten," by Mary McCarthy: pp. 209–211.

B35 "THE GENIAL HOST" 1963

WHEN WOMEN [*on the left of a double page opening; the rest is* en face:] LOOK AT MEN | An Anthology | Edited by | John A. Kouwenhoven | and Janice Farrar Thaddeus | Harper & Row, Publishers | New York, Evanston, and London | [*publisher's device*] [1963]

xxii, 437 pp., 2 leaves. 23½ × 15¾ cm. $7.50. Black cloth stamped in green on front cover and in gold and green on spine; mustard end-papers with publisher's device printed in white in an all-over pattern. Black and white dust-jacket lettered in orange, pink, black, and white.

5,000 copies were published on September 25, 1963. *On verso of title-page:* FIRST EDITION.

Contains "The Genial Host," by Mary McCarthy: pp. 104–120.

B36 "THE STONES OF FLORENCE" 1964

THE HUMANISTIC | TRADITION | *Edited by* | SARAH HERNDON | J. RUSSELL REAVER | The Florida State University | ROBERT F. DAVIDSON | St. Andrews Presbyterian College | WILLIAM RUFF | NATHAN COMFORT STARR | University of Florida | HOLT, RINEHART AND WINSTON | New York Chicago San Francisco [1964]

v–xii, 1–466 pp., with 4 plates between pp. 84–85, 180–181, 340–341, 404–405; 1 blank leaf. 22½ × 15¼ cm. $5.95. Rust paper over boards, lettered in black on front cover and on spine; end-papers. No dust-jacket.

Published on May 8, 1964.

Contains "The Stones of Florence," an excerpt from the book, by Mary McCarthy: pp. 324–334.

B37 "UNCLE MYERS" 1964

GERALD LEVIN | *The University of Akron* | prose | models | AN INDUCTIVE APPROACH TO WRITING | [*publisher's device*] *Harcourt, Brace & World, Inc.* | *New York and Burlingame* [1964]

x pp., 1 leaf, 278 pp. 21 × 14 cm. $2.95 (current price $3.25). White paper with wide and narrow stripes of light and dark green lettered in light and dark green and white.

First published on January 2, 1964, with four subsequent printings.

Contains "Uncle Myers," by Mary McCarthy: pp. 56–58, reprinted from *Memories of a Catholic Girlhood.*

B38 "THE MAN IN THE BROOKS BROTHERS SHIRT" 1964

STORY | AN INTRODUCTION | TO PROSE FICTION | edited by | ARTHUR FOFF | San Francisco State College | DANIEL KNAPP | San Francisco State College | WADSWORTH PUBLISHING | Belmont COMPANY California [1964]

x, 1–[435] pp., 1 blank leaf. 22½ × 15 cm. $3.25. White paper with pear-tree design in black on front and back covers; lettered in black and red on front cover and downward on spine.

10,000 copies were published on February 1, 1964, with two subsequent printings of 5,000 and 10,000 copies.

Contains "The Man in the Brooks Brothers Shirt," by Mary McCarthy: pp. 103–132.

B39 "CRUEL AND BARBAROUS TREATMENT" 1964

STUDIES IN FICTION | BLAZE O. BONAZZA CALIFORNIA | STATE COLLEGE AT FULLERTON | EMIL ROY UNIVERSITY OF SOUTHERN | CALIFORNIA | HARPER & ROW PUBLISHERS | NEW YORK, EVANSTON, AND LONDON [1964]

v–[viii] pp., 2 leaves, 3–[385] pp., 2 blank leaves. 23¼ × 15½ cm. $3.95. Brown paper lettered in black and white.

7,500 copies were published on December 30, 1964. There have been four subsequent printings of 5,000, 7,500, 10,213, and 5,000 copies, respectively.

Contains "Cruel and Barbarous Treatment," by Mary McCarthy: pp. 177–188.

B40 "THE UNSPOILED REACTION" 1964

THE | WORLDS OF | FICTION | Stories in Context | T. Y. GREET | *The Virginia Military Institute* | CHARLES E. EDGE | *University of North Carolina* | JOHN M. MUNRO | *University of Toronto* | *Houghton Mifflin Company · Boston* [1964]

vii–xiv pp., 1 leaf, 429 pp., 2 blank leaves. 21 × 14½ cm. $4.25 (paperback edition $2.50). Dark aqua buckram stamped in white on front cover and on spine; end-papers. No dust-jacket.

Published in 1964.

Contains "The Unspoiled Reaction," by Mary McCarthy: pp. 376–389.

B41 "CRUEL AND BARBAROUS TREATMENT" 1965

Interpreting | Literature | THIRD EDITION | [*publisher's device*] | K. L. KNICKERBOCKER | University of Tennessee | H. WILLARD RENIGER | State College of Iowa | HOLT, RINEHART AND WINSTON | New York · Chicago · San Francisco [1965]

iv–xviii pp., 1 leaf, 1–908 pp. 23¼ × 16½ cm. $6.95 (current price $7.75). Green and blue buckram stamped in blue, green, and white on front cover and on spine as follows: [*across, in blue*] KNICKERBOCKER | [*diamond in white*] | RENIGER | [*downward, in white on blue panel*] INTERPRETING LITERATURE | [*across, in blue*] THIRD EDITION | HOLT | RINEHART | WINSTON; end-papers. No dust-jacket.

First published on February 17, 1965.

Contains "Cruel and Barbarous Treatment," by Mary McCarthy: pp. 107–115.

B42 "ASK ME NO QUESTIONS" 1965

[*ornament*] | READ WITH ME | Selected by | THOMAS B. COSTAIN | Garden City, New York | DOUBLEDAY & COMPANY, INC. [1965]

xii pp., 3 leaves, 5–623 pp. 20¾ × 13½ cm. $5.95. Green imitation leather stamped in gold on spine; end-papers; top edges red. Gold, green, and white dust-jacket lettered in black, white, brown, and gold, with sketch of Costain in brown on front.

First published on May 7, 1965.

Contains "Ask Me No Questions," by Mary McCarthy: pp. 347–381.

B43 "A MEMORY OF A CATHOLIC GIRLHOOD" 1965

USES OF ENGLISH | WRITING | ABOUT ONESELF | Selected Writing | *Edited by* | ROBERT GARIS | WELLESLEY COLLEGE | D. C. HEATH AND COMPANY BOSTON | [*publisher's device*] [1965]

vii–x pp., 1 leaf, 1–143 pp., 2 blank leaves. 20¼ × 13½ cm. $1.50. White paper with design and lettering in mustard and red.

Published in January, 1965.

Contains "A Memory of a Catholic Girlhood," by Mary McCarthy: pp. 98–113, a reprinting of *"C'est le Premier Pas Qui Coûte."*

B44 "MISS GOWRIE" 1966

The ACT | of WRITING | and READING | A Combined Text | Alan Casty | Santa Monica City College | Prentice-Hall, Inc., Englewood Cliffs, N.J. [1966]

vi pp., 1 leaf, 266 pp. 27 × 19½ cm. $3.95. White paper with design in orange, brown, and black, lettered in black, white, and gray.

Published in 1966.

Contains "Miss Gowrie," by Mary McCarthy: pp. 181–182, a fragment from the chapter "The Figures in the Clock" in *Memories of a Catholic Girlhood.*

B45 "YELLOWSTONE PARK" 1966

IDENTITY | Stories for This Generation | Katherine Hondius | City College of San Francisco | Scott, Foresman and Company | Chicago Atlanta Dallas Palo Alto Fair Lawn, N.J. [1966]

xvii, 1–269 pp. 22½ × 15¼ cm. $2.95. White paper with geometric design in red on front cover and in black on back cover; lettered in black.

Published on January 2, 1966.

Contains "Yellowstone Park," by Mary McCarthy: pp. 200–216.

C

CONTRIBUTIONS BY MARY McCARTHY TO PERIODICALS[1]

[1] *Arranged chronologically.*
Contributions to a particular periodical are listed by reference number under the periodical in the index of titles.

C. Contributions to Periodicals

C1. Contrasts. *The Sampler* [Vassar College], (November 21, 1929), 5.

C2. Old-town. *The Sampler* [Vassar College], (November 21, 1929), 5.

C3. Touchstone Ambitious. *Vassar Journal of Undergraduate Studies,* VII (1933), 86–101.
A study of Sir John Harington.

C4. Two Crystal-Gazing Novelists. *Con Spirito,* I, 1 (February, 1933), 1–2.
A review of *Brave New World,* by Aldous Huxley, and *Public Faces,* by Harold Nicolson.
Unsigned, as are all the articles in this rebel Vassar publication, but recognized and identified by Miss McCarthy.

C5. In Pace Requiescamus. *Con Spirito,* I, 2 (April, 1933), 1–2.

C6. Pudding of Saints. *New Republic,* LXXV, 974 (August 2, 1933), 323.
A review of *A Calendar of Saints for Unbelievers,* by Glenway Wescott.

C7. Mr. Belloc's Theory of History. *Nation,* CXXXVIII, 3574 (January 3, 1934), 24–25.
A review of *Charles I,* by Hilaire Belloc.

C8. A Novel about the "Trouble." *Nation,* CXXXVIII, 3581 (February 21, 1934), 226.
A review of *Shake Hands With the Devil,* by Rearden Conner.

C9. [*A review of*] *The Young Manhood of Studs Lonigan.* By James T. Farrell. *Common Sense,* III, 3 (March, 1934), 29.

C10. Coalpit College. *New Republic,* LXXVIII, 1013 (May 2, 1934), 323.
A review of *I Went to Pit College,* by Lauren Gilfillan.

C11. A Novel of Distinction. *Nation,* CXXXVIII, 3595 (May 30, 1934), 626.
A review of *Bitter Bread,* by Nicolai Gubsky.

C12. Larger Than Life. *Nation,* CXXXVIII, 3596 (June 6, 1934), 655.
A review of *Magnus Merriman,* by Eric Linklater, and *Finnley Wren,* by Philip Wylie.

C13. Vivified History. *Nation,* CXXXVIII, 3597 (June 13, 1934), 679–680.
A review of *I, Claudius,* by Robert Graves.

C14. The Old South. *Nation,* CXXXIX, 3605 (August 8, 1934), 167–168.
A review of *So Red the Rose,* by Stark Young.

C15. Alexander the Eccentric. *Nation,* CXXXIX, 3606 (August 15, 1934), 194–195.
A review of *Alexander the Corrector,* by Edith Oliver.

C16. Mr. Burnett's Short Stories. *Nation,* CXXXIX, 3614 (October 10, 1934), 416–417.
A review of *The Maker of Signs,* by Whit Burnett.

C17. Romance of Paris. *Nation,* CXXXIX, 3625 (December 26, 1934), 746–747.
A review of *My Next Bride,* by Kay Boyle.

C18. Pass the Salt. *Nation,* CXL, 3630 (January 30, 1935), 137–138.
A review of *Lightship,* by Archie Binns; *February Hill,* by Victoria Lincoln; *Mary Peters,* by Mary Ellen Chase; and *Shipmates,* by Isabel Carter.

C19. One Man's Road. *Nation,* CXL, 3635 (March 6, 1935), 282, 284.
A review of *Personal History,* by Vincent Sheean.

C20. Living History. *Nation,* CXL, 3636 (March 13, 1935), 312–313.
A review of *The Black Consul,* by Anatoli Vinogradov.

C21. Two Novels About Musicians. *Nation,* CXL, 3638 (March 27, 1935), 366–367.
A review of *No Quarter Given,* by Paul Horgan, and *Cast Down the Laurel,* by Arnold Gingrich.

C22. Claudius as Emperor. *Nation,* CXL, 3640 (April 10, 1935), 424.
A review of *Claudius the God,* by Robert Graves.

C23. Miscellany. *Nation,* CXL, 3650 (June 19, 1935), 718, 720.
A review of *Blessed Is the Man,* by Louis Zara; *Ripeness Is All,* by Eric Linklater; *Susan and Joanna,* by Elizabeth Cambridge; *The Poacher,* by H. E. Bates; and *Jezebel's Daughter,* by A. R. Craig.

C24. An Old Battle. *Nation,* CXLI, 3654 (July 17, 1935), 82.
A review of *Fortune and Men's Eyes,* by George Cronyn.

C25. Young Gloom. *Nation,* CXLI, 3659 (August 21, 1935), 221.
A review of *Winter Orchard and Other Stories,* by Josephine Johnson.

C26. Tall Timber. *Nation,* CXLI, 3660 (August 28, 1935), 248–249.
A review of *Honey in the Horn,* by H. L. Davis.

C27. Middle Western Marriage. *Nation,* CXLI, 3661 (September 4, 1935), 278–279.
A review of *Dwell in the Wilderness,* by Alvah C. Bessie.

C28. Our Critics, Right or Wrong, Part I. *Nation,* CXLI, 3668 (October 23, 1935), 468–469, 472.

C29. ———, Part II: The Anti-Intellectuals. *Nation,* CXLI, 3670 (November 6, 1935), 542–544.

C30. ———, Part III. *Nation,* CXLI, 3672 (November 20, 1935), 595–596, 598.

C31. ———, Part IV: The Proletarians. *Nation,* CXLI, 3674 (December 4, 1935), 653–655.

C32. ———, Part V: Literary Salesmen. *Nation,* CXLI, 3676 (December 18, 1935), 717–719.
This series was written with Margaret Marshall.

C33. [A Letter to the Editor]. *Nation,* CXLII, 3678 (January 1, 1936), 18.
Written with Margaret Marshall.

C34. Saint Francesca of the Pacific Northwest. *Nation,* CXLII, 3680 (January 15, 1936), 82.
A review of *Marching! Marching!* by Clara Weatherwax.

C35. Minority Report. *Nation,* CXLII, 3688 (March 11, 1936), 326–327.
A review of *In Dubious Battle,* by John Steinbeck.

C36. Murder and Karl Marx. *Nation,* CXLII, 3690 (March 25, 1936), 381–383.

C37. Highbrow Shockers. *Nation,* CXLII, 3692 (April 8, 1936), 458–459.
A review of *Gaudy Night,* by Dorothy L. Sayers, and *The Crimson Patch,* by Phoebe Atwood Taylor.

C38. Two "Discoveries." *Nation,* CXLII, 3704 (June 27, 1936), 848.
A review of *Locos,* by Felipe Alfau, and *Village Chronicle,* by James McConnaughey.

C39. An Antique Genre. *Nation,* CXLIII, 2 (July 11, 1936), 52.
A review of *Waterloo,* by Manuel Komroff.

C40. Paris, 1848. *Nation,* CXLIII, 7 (August 15, 1936), 191–192.
A review of *Summer Will Show,* by Sylvia Townsend Warner.

C41. Circus Politics in Washington State. *Nation,* CXLIII, 16 (October 17, 1936), 442–444.

C42. [*A review of*] *Skutarevsky*. By Leonid Leonov. *Nation,* CXLIII, 20 (November 14, 1936), 584–585.

C43. [*A review of*] *Choose a Bright Morning*. By Hillel Bernstein. *Nation,* CXLIII, 22 (November 28, 1936), 641.

C44. [A Letter to the Editor]. *Nation,* CXLIII, 24 (December 12, 1936), 715–716.

C45. Our Actors and the Critics, Part I. *Nation,* CXLIV, 19 (May 8, 1937), 536+.

C46. The Actors and the Critics, Part II. *Nation,* CXLIV, 20 (May 15, 1937), 566–567.

C47. [*A review of*] *American Dream.* By Michael Foster. *Nation,* CXLV, 3 (July 17, 1937), 79–80.

C48. The Latest Shudder. *Nation,* CXLV, 12 (September 18, 1937), 296.
A review of *Seven Who Fled,* by Frederic Prokosch.

C49. [*A review of*] *The Return of Kai Lung*. By Ernest Bramah. *Nation,* CXLV, 17 (October 23, 1937), 454–455.

C50. Theater Chronicle. *Partisan Review,* IV, 1 (December 1937), 54–56.
Reprinted as "Two Bad Cases of Social Conscience" in *Sights and Spectacles.*

C51. Theater Chronicle. *Partisan Review,* IV, 2 (January, 1938), 48–49.
Reprinted as "Odets Deplored" in *Sights and Spectacles.*

C52. Versions of Shakespeare. *Partisan Review,* IV, 3 (February, 1938), 34–38.
Reprinted as "Elizabethan Revivals" in *Sights and Spectacles.*

C53. Theater Chronicle: Class Angles and Classless Curves. *Partisan Review,* IV, 5 (April, 1938), 52–56.
Reprinted as "Class Angles and a Wilder Classic" in *Sights and Spectacles.*

C54. Theater Chronicle: The Federal Theater Settles Down. *Partisan Review,* IV, 6 (May, 1938), 43–47.
Reprinted as "The Federal Theatre" [*sic*] in *Sights and Spectacles.*

C55. Theater Chronicle: New Sets for the Old House. *Partisan Review,* V, 1 (June, 1938), 41–44.
Reprinted as "Shaw and Chekhov" in *Sights and Spectacles.*

C56. The People's Choice. *Partisan Review,* VI, 1 (Fall, 1938), 106–110.

C57. Cruel and Barbarous Treatment. *Southern Review,* IV, 4 (Spring, 1939), 713–725.

C58. Two in Our Time. *Partisan Review,* VI, 4 (Summer, 1939), 111–114.
A review of *Adventures of a Young Man,* by John Dos Passos, and *The Bridegroom Cometh,* by Waldo Frank.

C59. Theater Chronicle: An Innocent on Broadway. *Partisan Review,* VII, 2 (March–April, 1940), 135–138.
Reprinted as "Saroyan, An Innocent on Broadway" in *Sights and Spectacles.*

C60. I Was There But I Didn't See It Happen. *New Republic,* CIII, 19 (November 4, 1940), 633–635.

C61. The Man in the Brooks Brothers Shirt. *Partisan Review,* VIII, 4 (July–August, 1941), 279–288, 324–343.

C62. Genial Host. *Southern Review,* VII, 2 (Autumn, 1941), 280–297.

C63. Ghostly Father, I Confess. *Harper's Bazaar,* LXXV, 2764 (April, 1942), 52–53+.

C64. Theater Chronicle: Chaos Is Come Again. *Partisan Review,* X, 1 (January–February, 1943), 82–83.
Reprinted as "The Skin of Our Teeth" in *Sights and Spectacles.*

C65. Theater Chronicle: The Russian Soul. *Partisan Review,* X, 2 (March–April, 1943), 184–186.
Reprinted as "The Russian Soul in Wartime" in *Sights and Spectacles.*

C66. Theater Chronicle: Broadway's Spring Offensive. *Partisan Review,* X, 3 (May–June, 1943), 279–280.

C67. Letter from New York. *Town and Country,* XCVIII, 4249 (July, 1943), 56+.

C68. Graham Greene and the Intelligentsia. *Partisan Review,* XI, 2 (Spring, 1944), 228–230.

C69. Theater Chronicle: Winter in the Theatre. *Partisan Review,* XI, 2 (Spring, 1944), 168–172.
Reprinted as "Wartime Omnibus" in *Sights and Spectacles.*

C70. C. Y. E. *Mademoiselle* (April, 1944), 112–113, 190–194.

C71. A Filmy Vision of the War. *Town and Country,* XCIX, 4259 (April, 1944), 72, 112.

C72. The Company Is Not Responsible. *New Yorker,* XX, 10 (April 22, 1944), 77–80.

C73. The Weeds. *New Yorker,* XX, 31 (September 16, 1944), 25–43.

C74. Theater Chronicle: We Must Have Faith. *Partisan Review,* XII, 1 (Winter, 1945), 90–92.

C75. Portrait of a Typical Negro? *New Leader,* XXVIII, 25 (June 13, 1945), 10.
A review of *Black Boy,* by Richard Wright.

C76. The Unspoiled Reaction, *Atlantic Monthly,* CLXXVII, 3 (March, 1946), 98–101.

C77. The Blackguard. *New Yorker,* XXII, 35 (October 12, 1946), 31–35.

C78. The Hiroshima "New Yorker." [A Letter] To the Editor. *politics,* III, 10 (November, 1946), 367.

C79. Lausanne. *Town and Country,* C, 4290 (November, 1946), 130+.

C80. Theater Chronicle: Dry Ice. *Partisan Review,* XIII, 5 (November–December, 1946), 577–579.
Reprinted with "The Farmer's Daughter" (C116) as "Eugene O'Neill–Dry Ice" in *Sights and Spectacles.*

C81. The Friend of the Family. *Town and Country,* CI, 4292 (January, 1947), 101+.

C82. Theater Chronicle: Gerontion. *Partisan Review,* XIV, 1 (January–February, 1947), 62–66.
Reprinted as "Five Curios" in *Sights and Spectacles.*

C83. Theater Chronicle: Something About the Weather. *Partisan Review,* XIV, 2 (March–April, 1947), 174–179.
Reprinted as "George Kelly" in *Sights and Spectacles.*

C84. Tyranny of the Orgasm. *New Leader,* XXX, 14 (April 5, 1947), 10.
A review of *Modern Woman, The Lost Sex,* by Ferdinand Lundberg and Marynia Farnham.

C85. Theater Chronicle: The Unimportance of Being Oscar. *Partisan Review,* XIV, 3 (May–June, 1947), 302–304.

C86. Theater Chronicle: What a Piece of Work Is Man! *Partisan Review,* XIV, 4 (July–August, 1947), 393–395.

C87. America the Beautiful: The Humanist in the Bathtub. *Commentary,* IV, 3 (September, 1947), 201–207.

C88. Theater Chronicle: Props and Property. *Partisan Review,* XV, 1 (January, 1948), 74–80.
Reprinted as "Four 'Well-Made' Plays" in *Sights and Spectacles.*

C89. The Cicerone. *Partisan Review,* XV, 2 (February, 1948), 151–176.

C90. Theater Chronicle: Oh, Sweet Mystery of Life. *Partisan Review,* XV, 3 (March, 1948), 357–360.
Reprinted as "A Streetcar Called Success" in *Sights and Spectacles.*

C91. Theater Chronicle: Modest Proposals. *Partisan Review,* XV, 4 (April, 1948), 477–480.
Reprinted as "Little Theatre" [*sic*] in *Sights and Spectacles.*

C92. Yonder Peasant, Who Is He? *New Yorker,* XXIV, 41 (December 4, 1948), 33–39.

C93. Gandhi. *politics,* V, 1 (Winter, 1948), 1–7.
Tributes to Gandhi by Mary McCarthy *et al.*

C94. Theater Chronicle: A Prince of Shreds and Patches. *Partisan Review,* XVI, 1 (January, 1949), 82–84.

C95. The Oasis. *Horizon,* XIX, 110 (February, 1949), 75–152.
Published before its appearance in book form.

C96. Theater Chronicle: Sartre and the McCoy, *politics,* VI, 1 (Winter, 1949), 49–51.

C97. Greenwich Village at Night, Part I. *New York Post* (February 21, 1950), 5, 20–21.

C98. ———, Part II. *New York Post* (February 22, 1950), 35.

C99. ———, Part III. *New York Post* (February 23, 1950), 5.

C100. ———, Part IV. *New York Post* (February 24, 1950), 67.

C101. ———, Part V. *New York Post* (February 26, 1950), 5, 20.

C102. ———, Part VI. *New York Post* (February 27, 1950), 35.

C103. ———, Part VII. *New York Post* (February 28, 1950), 45.

C104. ———, Part VIII. *New York Post* (March 1, 1950), 65.

C105. ———, Part IX. *New York Post* (March 2, 1950), 39.

C106. ———, Part X. *New York Post* (March 3, 1950), 65.

C107. The Old Men. *New Yorker,* XXVI, 13 (May 20, 1950), 28–34.

C108. Up the Ladder From *Charm* to *Vogue,* Part I. *Reporter,* III, 2 (July 18, 1950), 36–40.

C109. ———, Part II. *Reporter,* III, 3 (August 1, 1950), 32–35.

C110. Groves of Academe. *New Yorker,* XXVI, 50 (February 3, 1951), 28–32.
Reprinted, in revised form, as Chapter I of *The Groves of Academe.*

C111. The Vassar Girl. *Holiday,* IX, 5 (May, 1951), 46–55+.

C112. A Tin Butterfly. *New Yorker,* XXVII, 44 (December 15, 1951), 28–38.

C113. Mlle. Gulliver en Amérique. *Reporter,* VI, 2 (January 22, 1952), 34–37.

C114. C'est le Premier Pas Qui Coûte. *New Yorker,* XXVIII, 21 (July 12, 1952), 30–49.

C115. New Trends in American Education. *Listener* (July 24, 1952), 136–137.

C116. The Farmer's Daughter. *New York Times* (August 31, 1952), sec. 7, 7.
A review of *A Moon For the Misbegotten,* by Eugene O'Neill.
Reprinted, with "Dry Ice" (C80), as "Eugene O'Neill–Dry Ice" in *Sights and Spectacles.*

C117. Bard With Blood: Some Reflections on a Rare Presentation Opening the City Center Season. *New York Times* (February 1, 1953), sec. 7, 1, 3.
Reprinted as "The Little Gate" in *Sights and Spectacles.*

C118. The Figures in the Clock. *New Yorker,* XXIX, 2 (February 28, 1953), 24–32.

C119. Recalled to Life, or, Charles Dickens at the Bar. *Reporter,* VIII, 5 (March 3, 1953), 35+.
A review of *Charles Dickens: His Tragedy and Triumph,* by Edgar Johnson.

C120. Artists in Uniform. *Harper's Magazine,* CCVI, 1234 (March, 1953), 41–49.

C121. The Menace to Free Journalism in America. *Listener* (May 14, 1953), 791–792.

C122. The Revolt of the American Authors. *Listener* (November 26, 1953), 901–902.

C123. America the Beautiful. *Perspectives, USA,* II (Winter, 1953), 11–22.
Reprinted from *Commentary,* September, 1947.

C124. My Confession, Part I. *Reporter,* IX, 11 (December 22, 1953), 28–34.

C125. ———, Part II. *Reporter,* X, 1 (January 5, 1954), 27–31.
This two-part article was reprinted in *Encounter,* II, 2 (February, 1954), 43–56.

C126. Dottie Makes an Honest Woman of Herself. *Partisan Review,* XXI, 1 (January–February, 1954), 34–52.
Reprinted, with revision, as Chapter 3 of *The Group.*

C127. Settling the Colonel's Hash. *Harper's Magazine,* CCVIII, 1245 (February, 1954), 68–75.

C128. Thoughts of an American in England. *Listener* (June 17, 1954), 1041–1042.

C129. Appalachian Revolution. *New Yorker,* XXX, 30 (September 11, 1954), 40–63+.

C130. A Charmed Life. *New Yorker,* XXX, 34 (October 9, 1954), 36–44+.
Reprinted, with revision, as Chapter 1 of *A Charmed Life.*

C131. Letter From Portugal. *New Yorker,* XXX, 51 (February 5, 1955), 83–102.

C132. Theater Chronicle: Shaw at the Phoenix. *Partisan Review,* XXII, 2 (Spring, 1955), 252–259.
Reprinted as "Shaw Off Broadway" in *Sights and Spectacles.*

C133. The Family Tea Party. *Observer* (July 24, 1955), 13.

C134. Mister Rodriguez of Lisbon. *Harper's Magazine,* CCXI, 1263 (August, 1955), 65–70.

C135. September Morn. *New Yorker,* XXXI, 31 (September 17, 1955), 40–48.

C136. Yellowstone Park. *Harper's Bazaar,* LXXXIX, 2928 (November, 1955), 120–121+.

C137. The Will and Testament of Ibsen. *Partisan Review,* XXIII, 1 (Winter, 1956), 74–80.

C138. Profiles: The Revel of the Earth, Part I. *New Yorker,* XXXII, 20 (July 7, 1956), 27–30+.

C139. ———, Part II. *New Yorker,* XXXII, 21 (July 14, 1956), 29–30.

This two-part article was reprinted, with revision, in *Venice Observed.*

C140. Ask Me No Questions. *New Yorker,* XXXIII, 5 (March 23, 1957), 33–40+.

C141. Theater Chronicle: Sheep in Wolves' Clothing. *Partisan Review,* XXIV, 2 (Spring, 1957), 270–274.

C142. Naming Names, the Arthur Miller Case. *Encounter,* VIII, 5 (May, 1957), 23–25.

C143. A New Word. *Harper's Bazaar,* XCI, 2957 (April, 1958), 176–177+.

C144. The Vita Activa. *New Yorker,* XXXIV, 35 (October 18, 1958), 182–189.

A review of *The Human Condition,* by Hannah Arendt.

C145. An Academy of Risk. *Partisan Review,* XXVI, 3 (Summer, 1959), 476–480.

A review of *The Tradition of the New,* by Harold Rosenberg.

C146. Profiles: A City of Stone, Part I. *New Yorker,* XXXV, 25 (August 8, 1959), 36–38+.

C147. ———, Part II. *New Yorker,* XXXV, 26 (August 15, 1959), 32–34+.

C148. ———, Part III. *New Yorker,* XXXV, 27 (August 22, 1959), 38–42+.

This series was reprinted, with revision, in *The Stones of Florence.*

C149. Brunelleschi's Dome. *Harper's Bazaar,* XCII, 2974 (September, 1959), 206–209+.

C150. Theater Chronicle: Odd Man In. *Partisan Review,* XXVI, 1 (Winter, 1959), 100–106.

C151. The Fact in Fiction. *Partisan Review,* XXVII, 3 (Summer, 1960), 438–458.

C152. Exit a Conscience. [*London*] *Sunday Telegraph* (February 26, 1961), 6.
A review of *Resistance, Rebellion and Death,* by Albert Camus, and *The Collected Fiction of Albert Camus.*

C153. Characters in Fiction. *Partisan Review,* XXVIII, 2 (March–April, 1961), 171–191.

C154. Americans, Realists, Playwrights. *Encounter,* XVII, 1 (July, 1961), 24–31.
Published as " 'Realism' in the American Theatre" in *Harper's Magazine,* CCXXIII, 1334 (July, 1961), 45–52.
Reprinted as "The American Realist Playwrights" in *On the Contrary,* and *Mary McCarthy's Theatre Chronicles, 1937–1962.*

C155. Curtains for Tynan? *Observer* (October 22, 1961), 28.
A review of *Curtains,* by Kenneth Tynan.
Reprinted, with revision, as "Drapes" in *Partisan Review,* XXIX, 1 (Winter, 1962), 140–142, and in *Mary McCarthy's Theatre Chronicles, 1937–1962.*

C156. General Macbeth. *Harper's Magazine,* CCXXIV, 1345 (June, 1962), 35–39.

C157. A Bolt From the Blue. *New Republic,* CXLVI, 23 (June 4, 1962), 21–27.
A review of *Pale Fire,* by Vladimir Nabokov.
Reprinted, in slightly revised form, as "Nabokov's *Pale Fire*" in *Encounter,* XIX, 4 (October, 1962), 71–84.

C158. [A Letter to the Editor]. *New Republic,* CXLVII, 1 (July 2, 1962), 31.

C159. J. D. Salinger's Closed Circuit. *Harper's Magazine,* CCXXV, 1349 (October, 1962), 46–48.

C160. Drapes. *Partisan Review,* XXIX, 1 (Winter, 1962), 140–142.
A review of *Curtains,* by Kenneth Tynan.

C161. Déjeuner sur l'Herbe. *New York Review of Books,* "Special Issue" (1963), 4–5.
A review of *Naked Lunch,* by William Burroughs.
This was the first issue of *The New York Review of Books,* published in March, 1963.

C162. Burroughs' *Naked Lunch. Encounter,* XX, 4 (April, 1963), 92–98.

C163. Polly Andrews, Class of '33. *New Yorker,* XXXIX, 19 (June 29, 1963), 23–32+.
Reprinted, with revision, as Chapters 11 and 12 of *The Group.*

C164. The Hounds of Summer. *New Yorker,* XXXIX, 30 (September 14, 1963), 47–50+.

C165. Letter to a Translator. *Encounter,* XXIII, 5 (November, 1964), 69–71, 74–76.
Reprinted, in French, as "A propos du *Groupe:* Lettre à mon traducteur danois" in *Preuves,* XV, 174 (Août, 1965), 69–75.

C166. The Hue and Cry. *Partisan Review,* XXXI, 1 (Winter, 1964), 82–94.

C167. More on Eichmann. *Partisan Review,* XXXI, 2 (Spring, 1964), 253–284.
Commentary by Mary McCarthy *et al.*

C168. On Madame Bovary. *Partisan Review,* XXXI, 2 (Spring, 1964), 174–188.

C169. La littérature à la Mutualité. *Preuves,* XV, 168 (Février, 1965), 53–55.
Reprinted, in English, as "Crushing a Butterfly" in *Encounter,* XXIV, 3 (March, 1965), 53–55.

C170. Birds of America. *Southern Review,* I (New Series), 3 (July, 1965), 644–683.

C171. Verdict on Osborne. *Observer* (July 4, 1965), 17.
A review of *A Patriot for Me,* by John Osborne.

C172. Patriot or Coward. [A Letter to the Editor]. *Observer* (July 25, 1965), 26.

C173. Conversation Piece. *New York Times* (November 21, 1965), sec. 7, 5+.
An interview with Janet Flanner.

C174. Books of the Year: A Personal Choice. *Observer* (December 19, 1965), 22.
By Mary McCarthy *et al.*

C175. Nabokov. [A Letter to the Editor]. *New York Times* (July 10, 1966), sec. 7, 50.

C176. Everybody's Childhood. *New Statesman* (July 15, 1966), 90+.

A review of *The Opoponax,* by Monique Wittig.

C177. Old Men in a Hospital. *Nursing Clinics of North America,* I, 3 (September, 1966), 523–526.
Reprinted from *Cast a Cold Eye.*

C178. The Inventions of I. Compton-Burnett. *Encounter,* XXVII, 5 (November, 1966), 19–31.

C179. Books of the Year: Some Personal Choices. *Observer* (December 18, 1966), 23.
By Mary McCarthy *et al.*

C180. Report from Vietnam, Part I: The Home Program. *New York Review of Books,* VIII, 7 (April 20, 1967), 5–11.

C181. ———, Part II: The Problems of Success. *New York Review of Books,* VIII, 8 (May 4, 1967), 4–9.

C182. ———, Part III: Intellectuals. *New York Review of Books,* VIII, 9 (May 18, 1967), 21+.
Reprinted in *The Observer* (April 30, 1967), 11–12; (May 7, 1967), 11–12; (May 14, 1967), 21+.
The series was also reprinted in *Vietnam.*

C183. [A Letter to the Editors]. *New York Review of Books,* VIII, 12 (June 29, 1967), 29.

C184. Vietnam: Solutions. *New York Review of Books,* IX, 8 (November 9, 1967), 3–6.
Reprinted from *Vietnam.*

D

TRANSLATIONS INTO FOREIGN LANGUAGES OF BOOKS, STORIES, AND ARTICLES BY MARY McCARTHY

[1] *Arranged alphabetically by language and, within language groups, chronologically under the respective headings "Books" and "Periodicals."*

D. Translations into Foreign Languages

CZECH

BOOK:

D1. Smena, Publishing House of the Slovak Central Committee of the Youth Union, is planning to publish *Skupina,* a translation by Mrs. Eva Šimečková of *The Group,* in 1968.

DANISH

BOOKS:

D2. *Gruppen.* Fredensborg, Arena, Forfatternes Forlag A/S, January 10, 1964. 461 pp., 1 blank leaf. 21 × 13 cm. d.kr. 39.75. 6,000 copies. A translation, by Hans Hertel, of *The Group.*

D3. *Tværtimod.* Fredensborg, Arena, Forfatternes Forlag A/S, November 11, 1966. 245 pp., 1 blank leaf. 21 × 13 cm. d.kr. 32.75. 2,700 copies A translation, by Hans Hertel, of *On the Contrary.*

DUTCH

BOOKS:

D4. *Bohemiëns Zijn Ook Mensen.* Laren, A. G. Schoonderbeek, 1961. 1 leaf, 234 pp., 1 blank leaf. 20 × 14 cm. fl. 4.50. 700 copies. A translation, by H. S. Lanson, of *A Charmed Life.*

D5. *De Groep.* Leyden, A. W. Sijthoff's Uitgeversmaatschappij N.V., June, 1964. 367 pp., 1 blank leaf. 21 × 14 cm. fl. 12.90. 6,000 copies. A translation, by J. F. Kliphuis and Mrs. R. W. M. Kliphuis-Vlaskamp, of *The Group.*

D6. *De Groep.* Leyden, A. W. Sijthoff's Uitgeversmaatschappij N.V., November, 1965. 367 pp., 1 blank leaf. 20 × 13 cm. fl. 5.90. 12,500 copies. A translation, by J. F. Kliphuis and Mrs. R. W. M. Kliphuis-Vlaskamp, of *The Group.*

D7. *Herinneringen Aan Mijn Roomse Jeugd.* Amsterdam, N.V. De Arbeiderspers, November, 1966. 243 pp., 1 blank page, 3 leaves, 1 blank leaf. 19½ × 11½ cm. fl. 9.50. 3,000 copies. A translation, by Mrs. N. Brunt, of *Memories of a Catholic Girlhood.*

D8. *Eerste Persoon Meervoud.* Amsterdam, Polak & Van Gennep Uitgeversmaatschappij N.V., February 1, 1966. 276 pp. Dfl.

6.50. 4,000 copies. A translation, by Margaretha Ferguson, of *The Company She Keeps.*

FINNISH

BOOKS:

D9. *Rhymä.* Helsinki, Weilin & Göös, August, 1964. 426 pp., 3 blank leaves. 19¼ × 12¼ cm. Fmk. 13.50. 4,000 copies. A translation, by Antti Salomaa, of *The Group.* (3,000 additional copies were published in a second printing.)

D10. *Lumottu Elämä.* Helsinki, Weilin & Göös, October, 1965. 316 pp., 2 blank leaves. 19¼ × 12¼ cm. Fmk. 12.50. 3,000 copies. A translation, by Eila Pennanen and Aale Tynni, of *A Charmed Life.*

FRENCH

BOOKS:

D11. *Venise Connue et Inconnue.* Lausanne, Switzerland, Éditions de l'Œil, 1956. 223 pp., including plates. 48 NF. A translation, by Marcelle Sibon, of *Venice Observed.*

D12. *La Vie d'Artiste.* Paris, Librairie Plon, September, 1957. 9.90 f. 4,000 copies. A translation, by Denyse Meunier, of *A Charmed Life.*

D13. *Une Jeune Fille Sage.* Paris, Librairie Plon, April, 1959. 245 pp. 18 × 11 cm. 8.40 f. 3,500 copies. A translation, by Denyse Meunier, of *Memories of a Catholic Girlhood.*

D14. *Pierres de Florence.* Paris and Brussels, Éditions Sequoia, 1960. 74 leaves, 3–130 pp., 12 plates. 28 × 21 cm. 61 NF. 2,500 copies. A translation, by Jacques Houbart, of *The Stones of Florence.*

D15. *Dis-Moi Qui Tu Hantes.* Paris, Éditions Stock, June, 1963. 230 pp., 2 blank leaves. 20 × 14 cm. 16.50 f. 4,000 copies. A translation, by Angélique Levi, of *The Company She Keeps.*

D16. *Le Groupe.* Paris, Éditions Stock, February, 1965. 319 pp., 1 blank leaf. 22 × 15 cm. 16.20 f. 12,000 copies. A translation, by Antoine Gentien and Jean-René Fenwick, of *The Group.* (18,500 additional copies have been published in four subsequent printings.)

D17. *A Contre-Courant*. Paris, Éditions Stock, June, 1965. 6 leaves, 14–250 pp. 20 × 14 cm. 13.80 f. 5,000 copies. A translation, by Angélique Levi, of *On the Contrary*.

D18. *Mémoires d'une Jeune Catholique*. Paris, Société Nouvelle des Éditions Gonthier, April 22, 1966. [5]–249 pp., 3 leaves. 17¾ × 10¾ cm. 5.70 f. 15,000 copies. A translation, by Denyse Meunier and revised by Mary McCarthy, of *Memories of a Catholic Girlhood*.

GERMAN

BOOKS:

D19. *Florenz*. Gütersloh, C. Bertelsmann Verlag, 1960. 128 pp., plates. 28 × 22½ cm. DM 58. A translation, by Ursula Bethke, of *The Stones of Florence*.

D20. *Die Clique*. Munich, Droemersche Verlagsanstalt Th. Knaur Nachf., August, 1964. 5–439 pp. 20 × 12½ cm. DM 20. 270,-000 copies. A translation, by Ursula V. Zedlitz, of *The Group*. 30,000 copies were published in November, 1965, for Buchclub Ex Libris, Zurich, Switzerland.

D21. *Die Oase*. Munich, Droemersche Verlagsanstalt Th. Knaur Nachf., March, 1965. 7–132 pp., 5 leaves. 18 × 11½ cm. A paperback edition. DM 2.80. 16,500 copies. A translation, by Ursula V. Zedlitz, of *The Oasis*.

D22. *Sie Und Die Anderen*. Munich, Droemersche Verlagsanstalt Th. Knaur Nachf., August, 1965. 9–317 pp., 1 leaf. 13 × 12 cm. DM 16.80. 45,000 copies. A translation, by Rolf and Hedda Soellner, of *The Company She Keeps*.

D23. *Eine Katholische Kindheit*. Munich, Droemersche Verlagsanstalt Th. Knaur Nachf., March, 1966. 9–263 pp. 20 × 12½ cm. DM 15.80. 7,600 copies. A translation, by Maria Dessauer, of *Memories of a Catholic Girlhood*.

PERIODICALS:

D24. *Der Zauberkreis*. Serialized in *Die Welt* in the issues for February, 1966. A translation, by Maria Carlsson, of *A Charmed Life,* to have been published in book form by Droemersche in February, 1967.

D25. Yellowstone Park. *Annabelle,* March, 1966. A translation, by Maria Dessauer, of a chapter from *Memories of a Catholic Girlhood,* published before its appearance in book form.

D26. Geheimes, Gefährliches Selbst. *Der Spiegel,* 10 (February 27, 1967), 131–132. A translation of "The Inventions of I. Compton-Burnett."

D27. Nichts Wäre Schlimmer Als der Sieg, Part I. *Der Spiegel,* 29 (July 10, 1967), 79–92.

D28. ———, Part II. *Der Spiegel,* 30 (July 17, 1967), 67–81.

D29. ———, Part III. *Der Spiegel,* 31 (July 24, 1967), 60–72.

D30. ———, Part IV. *Der Spiegel,* 32 (July 31, 1967), 50–63. A translation, by Klaus Harpprecht, of "Report from Vietnam."

HEBREW

BOOK:

D31. *Ha-Hevra Vah Hi Mevalah.* Tel Aviv, Ziw, 1962. A translation, by Z. Deror and Etan Korngold, of *The Company She Keeps.* Published with *Omanut Ha-Nissuin Ha-Meušsarim,* a translation of *Cours de bonheur conjugal,* by André Maurois.

(Rights for *The Group* were granted to E. Kaiddar in 1965, but I have been unable to get any information on a Hebrew translation of this book.)

ITALIAN

BOOKS:

D32. *Vita Stregata.* Milan, Aldo Garzanti Editore, May, 1958. 2 leaves, 395 pp., 1 leaf. 20 × 13 cm. L. 1,700. A translation, by Carlo Rossi Fantonetti, of *A Charmed Life.*

Published also in a paperback edition in June, 1966, at L. 950.

D33. *Gli Uomini della Sua Vita.* Milan, Giangiacomo Feltrinelli Editore, July, 1962. 312 pp., 6 leaves. 20 × 12½ cm. L. 1,500. 3,800 copies. A translation, by Augusta Daré, of *The Company She Keeps.*

4,000 copies were published in a paperback edition in February, 1966, at L. 1,300.

D34. *Ricordi di un'Educazione Cattolica.* Verona, Arnoldo Mondadori Editore, November, 1963. 4 leaves, 10–443 pp.,

2 leaves. 19 × 11½ cm. L. 2,500. 3,049 copies. A translation, by Augusta Mattioli, of *Memories of a Catholic Girlhood.*
This edition includes "Al Contrario" on pp. 294–443, a translation, by Miss Mattioli, of selections from *On the Contrary.*

D35. *Il Gruppo.* Verona, Arnoldo Mondadori Editore, May, 1964. 5 leaves, 584 pp., 5 leaves. 19 × 11½ cm. L. 2,800. 44,238 copies. A translation, by Magda De Cristofaro, of *The Group.* (This edition has had seven additional printings.)

JAPANESE

BOOK:

D36. *Gurūpu.* Tokyo, Hayakawa Shobo Co., Ltd., October 31, 1964. 2 leaves, 3–412 pp., 7 leaves. 18¾ × 13 cm. 480 yen. 10,000 copies. A translation, by Toyoki Ogasawara, of *The Group.*

NORWEGIAN

BOOK:

D37. *Klikken.* Oslo, Gyldendal Norsk Forlag A/S, October 27, 1964. 7–316 pp., 3 leaves. 20¼ × 12¼ cm. kr. 29.50 and kr. 37.50. 5,000 copies. A translation, by Helge Simonsen, of *The Group.*

PORTUGUESE

BOOKS:

D38. *O Grupo.* Lisbon, Editôra Ulisseia Limitada, May, 1965. 463 pp. 18½ × 13 cm. 50$00. 3,000 copies. A translation, by Daniel Gonçalves, of *The Group.*

D39. *O Grupo.* Rio de Janeiro, Editôra Civilização Brasileira S.A., September 9, 1965, and July 8, 1966. 3 leaves, 379 pp. 21 × 14 cm. Cr$3,000 (first printing), Cr$5,000 (second printing). 4,000 copies in each printing. A translation, by Fernando de Castro Ferro, of *The Group.*

D. Translations into Foreign Languages

SPANISH

BOOK:

D40. *El Grupo*. Mexico City, Editorial Joaquin Mortiz, November 24, 1966. 7–389 pp., 3 blank leaves. 15 × 9 cm. 50 pesos. 4,000 copies. A translation, by Carmen Rodríguez De Velasco and Jaime Ferrán, of *The Group*.

(Rights for *The Group* originally went to Editorial Seix Barral, S.A., Barcelona, but the book was denied a censorship seal in Spain. Seix Barral was to have published a Spanish translation of *On the Contrary* in Spring, 1967, with a deletion, by the censorship office, of "a line and a half on page 127." The line in question is quite possibly: "General Franco's regime already appears superannuated beside the Estado Novo," from "Letter From Portugal.")

SWEDISH

BOOK:

D41. *Gruppen*. Stockholm, Albert Bonniers Förlag AB, 1964. 5–362 pp. 22 × 14 cm. Sw.Crs. 29:50 (paperback), Sw.Crs. 36:00 (hard cover). 7,360 copies plus 430 copies for Finnish distribution. A translation, by Harriet Alfons and Jadwiga P. Westrup, of *The Group*.

YUGOSLAVIAN

BOOK:

D42. Otokar Kersovani, Rijeka, has rights for *The Group,* which it was to have published in 1967. The book had been scheduled for publication in 1966, but the translation proved to be unsatisfactory.

E

APPENDIX: MISCELLANEA

E. Appendix: Miscellanea

E1. INTERVIEWS WITH MARY MC CARTHY

a. The Art of Fiction XXVII: Mary McCarthy. Elisabeth Niebuhr, *Paris Review,* XXVII (Winter–Spring, 1962), 59–94.

Reprinted in *The Paris Review: Writers at Work, Second Series* (New York: Viking Press, 1963), 283–315, and in *The Writer's Yearbook,* XXXV (1964), 10–15+.

b. Mary McCarthy Said:. P. D. Smith, *Vogue,* CXLII, 7 (October 15, 1963), 98–99+.

c. Mary McCarthy Ad-Libs on Shakespeare's Women and Sundry Matters: A Show Soliloquy. *Show,* IV, 2 (February, 1964), 93+.

E2. A BOOK CO-EDITED BY MARY MC CARTHY

KALTENBORN | EDITS THE NEWS | EUROPE—ASIA—AMERICA | by H. V. Kaltenborn | [*publisher's device*] | MODERN AGE BOOKS, INC., NEW YORK [1937]

5 leaves, iii–xiii, 1–183 pp. 19¼ × 13¾ cm. $0.35 ($0.85 in hardbound edition). Paper with photograph of Kaltenborn on front cover; sewn. On recto of unnumbered page following dedication page and preceding Table of Contents:

ACKNOWLEDGMENTS

> The author's thanks are due to Roger Paul Craig and Mary McCarthy for valuable editorial assistance, to the Columbia Broadcasting System for permission to reproduce from *Talks,* material broadcast from Spain and to *The Commentator* for permission to use source material and excerpts from my recent articles.

Miss McCarthy informs me that she and Roger Craig were, in fact, the ghost writers of the book.

E3. TRANSLATIONS BY MARY MC CARTHY

a. The 27th of September. *Partisan Review,* III, 2 (March, 1936), 19–21.

A translation from the French of André Gide.

b. Second Thoughts on the U.S.S.R. *Partisan Review,* IV, 2 (January, 1937), 21–28.
A translation from the French of André Gide.
This unsigned translation was identified by Miss McCarthy.

c. The Iliad, or, The Poem of Force. *politics,* II, 11 (November, 1945), 321–331.
A translation from the French of Simone Weil.
Reprinted, in 1947, as *politics Pamphlet No. 1,* and, in 1956, as *Pendle Hill Pamphlet No. 91* (Wallingford, Pa.).

d. Eye for Eye. *politics,* IV, 4 (July–August, 1947), 134–140.
A translation from the French of Simone de Beauvoir.

e. *On the Iliad.* New York: Pantheon Books, 1947.
A translation from the French of Rachel Bespaloff.

f. Sartre and the Prize. *Encounter,* XXIV, 2 (February, 1965), 55–57.
A translation from the Italian of Nicola Chiaromonte.

E4. BRAILLE AND RECORDED EDITIONS OF BOOKS BY MARY MC CARTHY

The dates given note when permission was granted to braille, or record, the particular books. (Titles are listed alphabetically.) Unless specifically noted as tape or recording, the editions are in braille.

a. CAST A COLD EYE
Chicago Public Library, December 1, 1950.
Library of Congress, March 4, 1964.

b. A CHARMED LIFE
Library of Congress, November 21, 1955, and September 8, 1964.

c. THE GROUP
Best Selling Books for the Blind, Inc., November 19, 1963. Permission was granted to record the book.
American Printing House for the Blind, April 3, 1964.
Students Braille Library, May 18, 1964. Permission was granted to braille one copy of the book.
Library of Congress, June 25, 1964. Permission was granted to tape the book.

d. THE GROVES OF ACADEME
Library of Congress, March 26, 1964, and February 7, 1966.

e. MEMORIES OF A CATHOLIC GIRLHOOD
Students Braille Library, June 24, 1964.

INDEX OF TITLES

Index of Titles

Index of Titles

Index of Titles

Index of Titles

Index of Titles

Index of Titles

INDEX OF NAMES

Index of Names
(PERSONS, PUBLISHERS, ETC.)

Index of Names

Index of Names

Index of Names